How Can I Be a Leader?

TAKING CIVIC ACTION

Melissa Raé Shofner

CIVICS FOR THE REAL WORLD™

Rosen Classroom™

People look up to good leaders. How can I be a leader?

I set a good example for others.
I read quietly at my desk.

I raise my hand and wait my turn. This gives everyone a chance to talk.

I say "please" and "thank you."
This shows people that I care.

I work hard in school.
Learning is important to me.

I believe in myself. I always smile. This makes me a leader.

WORDS TO KNOW

desk

hand

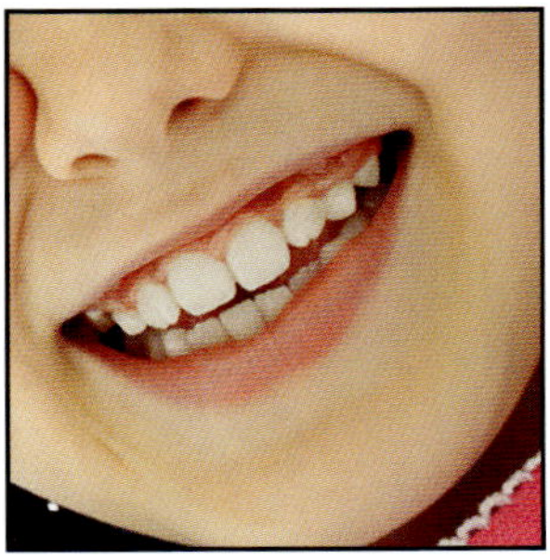

smile